AF355445

WORDS OF WANDERER

Echoes from journey of emotions

JATIN DADHICH

BookLeaf
Publishing

India | USA | UK

Copyright © JATIN DADHICH
All Rights Reserved.

This book has been self-published with all reasonable efforts taken to make the material error-free by the author. No part of this book shall be used, reproduced in any manner whatsoever without written permission from the author, except in the case of brief quotations embodied in critical articles and reviews.

The Author of this book is solely responsible and liable for its content including but not limited to the views, representations, descriptions, statements, information, opinions, and references ["Content"]. The Content of this book shall not constitute or be construed or deemed to reflect the opinion or expression of the Publisher or Editor. Neither the Publisher nor Editor endorse or approve the Content of this book or guarantee the reliability, accuracy, or completeness of the Content published herein and do not make any representations or warranties of any kind, express or implied, including but not limited to the implied warranties of merchantability, fitness for a particular purpose.
The Publisher and Editor shall not be liable whatsoever...

Made with ❤ on the BookLeaf Publishing Platform
www.bookleafpub.in
www.bookleafpub.com

Dedication

"This collection is offered first in reverence to God, Sri Guru Babaji, and Sukhramdas ji Babaji, my masters. It is through their boundless grace that I exist and possess the insight to navigate the depths of my emotions. Their influence has shaped my life, revealing that every seemingly ordinary moment holds profound meaning, inviting us to explore beyond the surface. They instilled in me the spirit of a wanderer, urging me to search for what transcends mere existence.

My deepest gratitude extends to my parents, grandparents, and family, whose unwavering support nurtured not only my writing, but the very essence of my being. Their unique blend of friendship and parental guidance illuminated the truth that emotions are not obstacles, but pathways on a journey of self-discovery, a journey we must all undertake.

And finally, this book is dedicated to the silent explorers of the heart, to those who have experienced the vast spectrum of human feeling. It is a testament to the journey through the ever-shifting tides of emotion, a voyage through the constellations of the soul. May these poems serve as a beacon, guiding you through darkness and illuminating the stars within. May they be a map, a compass, and, more importantly, a companion on your emotional journey. In the shared experience of feeling, we find connection, understanding, and the strength to navigate the ever-changing landscapes within. Though everyone embarks on this journey alone, thank you for choosing me as a companion.".

Preface

"We are all wanderers on this path, navigating the intricate terrain of our inner selves. Some paths are well-worn, familiar, and comforting. Others are overgrown, shrouded in doubt and fear. Yet, each step, each stumble, each breath taken along the way shapes us, refines us, and ultimately, reveals the strength and resilience that resides within.

This book is an invitation to feel, to reflect, and to recognize the universality of our emotional landscapes. It is a reminder that even in the darkest corners of our hearts, there is light to be found, and that the journey, in all its complexity, is where true beauty lies.

It is a glimpse into the realization that life, from before birth to beyond death, is a fleeting existence, a series of breaths. We are often mere shadows, unaware of our own being. These poems chart the journey of a wanderer through the rollercoaster of emotions, a quest to find true home and purpose, to truly live rather than merely exist.

May these poems be a companion on your own emotional voyage, a gentle hand to hold as you explore the depths of your heart. When you dare to look inward, to embark on this journey, and to traverse these emotions, may these poems connect you to the shared human experience, assuring you that you are not alone."

Acknowledgements

This book would not exist without the unwavering support of my parents, who fostered a creative haven for its blossoming. I am deeply indebted to my family, teachers, and friends who offered their insightful feedback, unwavering belief, and quiet encouragement. They helped me nurture my love for writing poetry, which, over time, became my greatest escape and favorite habit. Reading this, I hope you feel the depth of my gratitude. You helped me not only continue this habit but also guided me to take it to the next level. My sincere gratitude goes to the friend who first sparked my passion for writing, and to the poet Rumi, whose poems profoundly influenced my work. Additionally, I extend a heartfelt thank you to Book Leaf Publishing's Write Angle Challenge. I never imagined my book would be published so early in my journey. Finally, I extend a heartfelt thanks to all who graciously gifted me the time, space, and support necessary to bring this collection to fruition."

Who Are You

"The way you saw me,
I felt lost,
Within my firm isolation,
I felt contrast.

A strange sound began resonating within me,
compelling me to pull out,
confined within these reveries,
"Who are you?" I'm eager to figure out.

Do away with my disguise,
I came out,
looked down the evenfall,
casting off my tenebrosity.
You, standing at the horizon,
like a glimpse of eternity,
my eyes envisioning the wonder,
"Who are you?" I'm fervid to find out.

Beside the river of love,
I'm longing for a drink,
mounted the enlightened peak,
finally, I stand upon the brink.
It's a reflection splitting in illusions,
clearing all my confusions.
Now there is no mist,
I feel you, you're the last,
amid these worldly temptations,
only your manifestation outlasts.

It's you who pervades everywhere,
like thoughts in a tranquil mind,
after devoting my life in search of you,
I recognized you and forgot who I was."

It's Time I Should Hug My Shadows...

"It's time I should hug my shadows,
they can't bear this pain anymore,
bound in shackles of vows,
yearning for waves standing at shore.
Their eyes stinging with unshed tears,
covering the wounds I cannot restore,
no matter how dark, they stand for me,
till day breaks and I'm ready to explore.

These reflections which I follow,
they love me less and hurt me more,
the desire to relive those moments of past,
to slip into those ripped clothes I never wore,
to stay in that house I never owned,
I wish I would have,
never stepped outside that backdoor,
but I bear this unfortunate agony,
of being deserted by all I sought before.

I lost myself in the depth of those tears,
what's left is a place I've always searched for,
these illusions don't let my shackles loose,
but my soul dragged me back from my heart's core.
Now I should stop the war within,
"I can still raise the sword, but what for?"

These emotions will revive again,
but my eyes cannot weep blood for every bone,
or they'll run dry,
it's time I should hug my shadows,
for without me, they surely die."

This lonely way...

"Fear not this loneliness,
it shall not haunt you long.
When your own screams you hear,
their echoes find the place where you belong.

These quiet rooms,
they talk a lot.
You don't listen to them,
they exist, though you forgot.

Silence hurts.
A shadow breaks.
You cry for what you feel,
just forgive all your mistakes.

Be grateful for the loneliness.
It washed you, like a pearl freed from sand.
Now, you see yourself.
Now, you hold your own hand.

It's simple, just follow your breath, it knows the way,
soothing your heart, no matter how hard the day.
Celebrate this moment, before its beauty pales.
Feel your true self, with every inhale.
Forget who was ever with you,
as with you, you always stay.
You'll find yourself soon,
just never step off this lonely way."

The Rooftop

"For me, this rooftop,
Is no less than a temple,
Where I often visit,
Whenever my heart starts to tremble.

A haven where the city's clamor fades,
A place where mind speaks with my soul,
These sunsets mirror my scream,
When I throw this facade
And relinquish every role.

How much hollow I'm behind this face,
This world under me, does not know,
These cold winds pass through me,
Sweeping my frozen tears that long to flow.

A flickering light, in night's embrace,
Emotions bloom, with shifting trace,
Anger, grief, and joy's release,
I break them free, on this rooftop's peace.

Where starlight darkens, on this lonely height,
My soul breathes hope, till dawn's soft light,
This place absorbs my despair,
Bestowing a tranquil mental space,
It's more than a rooftop,
It's my therapy,
The reason for my smiling face."

The Gilded Cage of Needs

"These walls, a cold, bleak jail,
it traps my soul.
These looming skyscrapers,
they always seek control.
Their shadows stretch, a concrete blight,
stealing the sun, and dimming my light.
The air is thick with unspoken fears,
echoing whispers through passing years.

The illusory light of fame,
lures like an oasis,
cuffing me in shackles of desire,
exploiting me in times of crisis.
They snatch my freedom,
leaving me in a golden cave.
From the window, seeing birds fly,
I realize I'm not even that brave.

Within these gilded bars,
sorrow lingers, sadness stays.
I wish to borrow wings from those birds,
to feel the soft wind brush golden rays.
I want to fly, to my home,
where a year seems like a day.
A melodic whistle that calls me,
from the woods far away.

Where my heart tranquilly resides,
in nature's hush, my soul hides.
Where scent of flowers heals you from inside,
where your future nature decides.
Raw trails, where bare feet find dancing toes,
where stars spread over sky like a beautiful rose.
The flow of life, this river shows.
Mesmerizing silence these valleys knows.

That place is my home,
where I can only dream to go.
For I'm a prisoner of my needs,
a heavy truth that hurts to know.
This gilded cage fulfills my fantasy,
but restricts my happiness to flow.

More than I ask, they ever give,
yet I feel no real gain.
A sweet poison creeping through my veins,
inviting death, with unbearable pain.
Like senses numbed by bitter cold,
they trapped my dreams in cage of gold.
I want to fly, and break these chains,
but I wonder, will I ever see my home again?

Got My Lenses Up

"It was first time,
Got my lenses up,
Since I was nine,
Senses caught me up.
Everyone around me changed,
All strange but unexplained.
Can see dual faces around,
Blurred images, no sight profound.
Why, what, how, my mind can't cope up,
Hence, I got my lenses up!

Now I can see it all clear,
Lie in truth, courage in fear.
Images set has different frames,
Love, anger, jealousy and many are their names.
Now I see images that blurred,
Expectations from others got me disturbed.
Moods are frames that affect me a lot,
Eccentric image each one got.
I can't paint myself according to all,
So I painted mine, the one for all.
Just like minds ahead of heart,
Four frames, two to love and two to outsmart.

Although foggy emotions cover the lenses,
But after a while I just clear it up.
Now frames don't get my mind blurred,
Even at lowest my hope is up.
I remember it was the first time,
I got my lenses up!"

It's Fear

"Butterflies rolling down my belly,
breaths freezing slowly,
hands slip in the heart's lost place,
nerves frail, in a frantic chase.

Every second tearing me apart,
is it fear grabbing my heart?
One asked, "What's the fear?"
Struck in silence, I replied,

"This is not just fear,
These are haunting thoughts behind my tears!"
Thoughts of losing, failing, not fitting, trapped inside,
This feeling of being stuck where my dreams have died.

Terrible burden of standing upon expectations,
anxiety about overcoming bad situations.
Amid this hurricane, I'm drowning,
can't go up, but still grinding.

This is fear haunting my identity,
but also strengthening my integrity.
Can't see anything, but I'm going,
fear is the sign I'm growing.

It threatens me, it's a scary imagination,
believe me, it's fear that guides me to my destination!"

Knot

"Knot, a beautiful bond,
holding together two distinct ends,
a nexus of love,
resting two worlds hand in hand.

It's the tapestry of stars,
where destinies align,
where one becomes a cosmic mirror,
in which the other's reflection shines.

A knot of love is not a jaunt,
it's a journey forged into a heart of stone,
to live up to it, you have to be real,
staking every breath on what's been known.

A knot is a relationship,
between our entwined souls,
the harder fate may pull,
the tighter it holds.

Sadly, to find release,
people untie these knots,
they even silence their own voice,
just to listen to the whisper of their own thoughts.

But they bear no blame,
for time unfolds as it may,
a curse, each knot,
is destined to burn one day.

After a certain time,
these ends will part their way,
embrace these bonds, a sacred boon,
later you might crave, but these roles you cannot play.

Eventually, this world grows still, your memories will
sway,
in lonely depths, you slowly fade away."

Sound Of Heart...

"The sound of heart,
a rhythm soul plays,
our forlorn feelings,
reminding us of those days.

When the world is hushed in silence,
we witness that exotic wave,
strings of thought weave a divine chord,
they manifest the piece we most crave.

This universe, our own reflection,
why then, should we fear?
Memories, the songs we composed,
old albums, we love to hear.

Let your sick heart beat on,
let the old man journey his way,
fear not, he's known these trails well,
just set his inner child free,
let him find his play."

Escape...

"Escape this cage of illusions,
don't lock your reality within.
Grasp the sunray of hope,
leave darkness, let new light begin.

Witness life's serene embrace,
healing you with every breath.
Don't be fooled by fleeting grace,
wake up, you are more than death.

Don't fear this change,
it comes for all one day.
Let go of those alluring dreams,
they were never meant to stay.

Hug yourself, love yourself,
let forgiveness pave your way.
Don't stake your soul for them,
step off their worn-out pathway.

Break these shackles of emotions,
fear not the loss, the fading sight.
Your journey's dawn, not this endless night.
Let blessings rise, in vibrant hue,
and bloom within the land of you."

Highway....

"Life's a highway, swift and wide,
those who grasp its endless stride,
understand life's fleeting grace,
time's relentless, hurried chase,
fuels a shift to faster lanes,
a frantic rush through life's domains.

It's a long way,
where people pause for joy and tears,
they embrace their destiny's sway,
by raising a glass to golden years.

This life, a highway's harsh design,
no pause for those who reach their line,
accidents occur, a truth we know,
death's final journey, spirits undergo.
The highway whispers its farewell,
to every friend, beneath its spell.

Survivors, reborn, embrace the change,
they shape their fate, and rearrange,
they seek for meaning, clear and bright,
where shadows vanish into light.
New hope they find with every dawn,
life's highway rolls, forever on."

I Want to Forget You...

"I want to forget you,
Just the way I loved you,
Your smile, your deep eyes,
Everything that reminds me of you.
That rooftop, where I found you,
Lost among the stars,
All those moments we spent,
Etched as scars.

I want to forget,
The touch of your warm breath,
Your soothing soft hands,
I swore to hold till death.
Those drawn-out talks,
A timeless wish to never stray,
Sitting beside bonfires, for hours drawn long,
Holding back the night from yesterday's sway.

*"I want to forget,
Your essence,
Imprinted on my soul.
I want to forget those fake promises,
The lies I held, beyond what I could bear.
I want to tear,
Your threads from me,
As you severed mine.
I want to forget your nearness, a shadow,
To find myself,
and disappear."*

Take a step..

"Take a step,
Even if you don't see the light ahead,
Take a step,
Even if you feel like you're drop dead,
Take a step,
Even if your world is falling apart,
Take a step,
Even if it is tearing your heart,
Take a step,
Even if there is no one to hold your hand,
Take a step,
Even if your journey is going to end,
Take a step,
Even if you cannot run that fast,
Take a step,
Even if it is your last,
Take a step,
For what it may,
Just take a step,
To grow, it is the only way."

Life Is Not Pause and Play...

"Please hold more of me,
or let me let go a little of you.
For which I can't leave,
for which you choose not to stay.
Remember the note that binds us,
whose sound no longer resonates.
Don't pull the strings apart,
the farther you move, our tone fades.
Once strings are broken,
they'll never be the same,
like you promised we'd stay together,
now you barely recall my name.

I gave you my heart,
my feelings you betrayed.
You came as a rising sun,
and set upon a mountain of despair.
The habit I had of being alongside you,
since you left, there is an aching void beyond repair.

I still bear the scars that your silence gave,
I let them burn hoping they'll have mercy someday.
You put a pause to "us,"
now only you blithely stay.
As I'm trapped in a reminiscence loop,
where I can only hate you till my feelings decay.

Spring is over, autumn is here,
leaves fall, and no one cares.
It's natural to forget,
but it's not as easy as they portray.
We have to cut mountains,
just to ensure a way.
The thing we had was real,
but with time, even real fades.
The rhythm you left practicing,
eventually, you'll forget to play.
What's gone is gone,
not even angels can put it back the same way.
Someday, you'll wake up,
and realize it's too late for anything to say.
No matter how hard you try,
the truth is, life is not a pause and play."

Scars I Bear...

"Each scar I bear,
Has its own story,
Some hurt for defeats,
Some shine for glory.

They remind me of those battles,
How fiercely each one I fought,
How my darkness sustained me,
When all else came to naught.

This beautiful life's vulnerability,
Is what these brutal battles taught.
That someday, life's chaos yields to stillness,
Is a truth my heart has barely caught.

I embrace these scars, they are the proof,
Where others faltered, I dared to be brave,
These years unveiled the truth of my existence,
Now my scars fade, life's essence I take,
And seek my quiet grave."

It Was Too Late to See...

*"After a long time,
it's in front of his eye,
a castle of dreams,
for which he's ready to die,
made out of sand,
with love in its every end,
a paradisiacal wonderland,
built with his own hand.*

*Upon the roof, his pride did soar,
he felt no fear, and asked for more,
he used the weak, and slammed the door,
on any soul he found a bore.
His truth was his, and his alone,
his dreams were his, upon his throne,
but he didn't care, what he had sown.*

Lured by lust, by ego's need,
he sowed his seed in cycles of greed.
He scorned the grace, the humble creed,
forgot the shelter, once was his only deed.
Though blessings flowed, a gilded stream,
he owned them not, a fleeting dream.

For one above, with watchful eye,
his justice falls, where truths lie.
A tidal wave, a sudden blow,
erased his reign, in sorrow's flow.
From lauded name, to whispered plea,
he stood in shock, as it was too late to see."

The 'I' Won When 'I' Died

"After a dark night,
again this sky glows,
just to rip apart everything,
this night knows.
Dawn smiles for the healings,
he knows now there'll be no sorrow,
dusk cries for the feelings,
as for them there'll be no tomorrow.

To get what we want,
we have to walk through pain,
no one blames the voice of the heart,
but it needs to stop or else go vain.
Walking down the memory lane,
there's a life we still seek,
strenuous paths we chose,
but we were too weak.

The warrior looks at a mirror,
he stirs inner throes, a haunted tier,
the reflection heard a crestfallen whisper,
'Do or die' is the only game twister.
He picked the sword,
slayed the mirror into pieces,
he walked to the throne,
now there's no one he misses.

Once in a while this battle every warrior fights,
to make sure there's no one to hold him aside.
Day won and Night cried,
the 'I' won when 'I' died.."

I Don't Stand in the Same Shoes Everyday

"They bear my burden, like no one can,
their darkened surface, where my trials land,
from mountain rocks to dunes of sand,
through muddy fields, or barren, rocky land.
They never ask why,
no matter where I stand,
they carry me everywhere,
where my life commands.

They offer this unwavering trust,
a bond beyond compare,
for me they unhesitatingly plunge into mire's embrace,
so I can savor every journey of which my heart's aware.
They rise like whispers from dust below,
to tender my mind's comfort, love and care,
they walk along with me those uncharted roads,
visiting them alone, I would hardly dare.
These rough scratches they've got,
they continue this journey enfolding them,
they endure all the harshness of nature,
to let me enjoy this beauty without cursing them.

They learn from yesterday's covered trails,
and pave new pathways for the next day.
They are those faithful companions,
who stand till their own light begins to fray.
This never-ending quest for my existence,
journeys where my adventurous spirit long to stay.
Imagine walking roads of thoughts,
and watch them all end my destined way.
Yet they fill me with the hope of sunrise,
which drags my soul to listen what they say.
I fall, I cry, I rise, I run, but I don't stand
in the same shoes everyday."

Just Walk...

"There's nothing wrong,
To walk the existing line,
To follow a path,
Where you know you'll be fine.

It's the journey itself,
Not the path you pave,
It's about attaining,
Your deepest crave.

Reaching those peaks,
Sitting in caves,
Embracing the wonders,
Listening to the waves.

It's a never-ending quest,
You walk till your grave,
To reach your desires,
These paths are simply all you have.

Do not always seek new ways,
Not everything must have your name,
Do not stop, just keep walking,
If time runs short, the fault is yours to claim.
Think about all you have strived for,
If you failed to reach, your efforts will go in vain.
Just walk, keeping your emotions close,
Before it's too late, to be late ever again."

How You Earned Your Shining Greys

"Live it as you want,
like the old man says,
I skip the well-worn trails,
for I love to find my own ways.
It's a rugged pathway,
where nature's soft gaze gently sways.
Sunrays shower blessings through the canopy,
like a heavenly ray showing you the ways.

A stream flows beside,
never stops but forever stays.
It's you who want to hold things in love,
otherwise, nature has its own way to embrace.
Listen to these bugs and birds,
their melody never fails to amaze.
It's so pleasing to feel how it all exists,
imagine being in eternal love that'll never erase.

If you worry about falling leaves
and breaking branches,
you'll miss what truly stays.
The present is a divine pleasure,
but it demands surrender to its every phase.
You'll never be a wanderer,
if you're too vainglorious to accept.
Every morning you're nothing but just a naive.
If the old refuse to go,
how will the new one take its place?
If you never start this journey,
you'll be full of regrets standing in your lonely space.

People often lose their spirit,
from fear of losing paths within the maze.
Surviving life's rollercoaster is a real adventure,
after all, you'll feel your heartbeat raise.
Don't fear your adventures,
they'll give you those awesome days.
Even if you end up with nothing,
you'll still have your story,
about how you earned your shining greys."

Love is true, lover is myth

"It's the purest thing,
One can feel,
A treasure found,
No one can steal.
It's love,
That makes me lost in those eyes,
It's love,
That bids my soul to rise.

It's everywhere,
Till I want to know it,
It's gone,
When I want to hold it.
It's a serene flow,
The whole universe within me,
But it stops,
When I reduce it to just you and me.

When I say, 'I love you,'
I love every part of you,
That stays within me,
From every sip I take of you,
To each drop,
That I let go of me,
We stay forever until eternity,
Leaving behind the forms,
We loved in,

Though our world may end,
Our whispers continue to echo,
Being as one, we do not fade with it.

Don't seek for an answer,
Simply close your eyes and believe,
For love is true, lover is a myth."

A Falling Raindrop...

"Cold stormy night,
I was full of despair,
sad and huddled under my blanket,
cursing this world for not being fair.
Darkness veiled my mind,
reality warped into a gloomy delusion everyone fears.
Suddenly I glanced outside my window,
and a wonder took hold.
That fleeting moment swept me off course,
to a sanity my darkness could hardly bear.

It was a moment when the raindrops
fall upon a reflecting surface.
The falling drop and its mirrored twin,
both gushing to settle themselves as one,
so driven by instinct,
they gradually blend together.
In their shared resemblance they realize,
where they were rushing to reach,
was what they already were.

Seeking oneness they found void,
with their essence lost in loops of time.
They pulled their hands out to be one,
both vanished in serenity,
their memories being forever undone.

Just like these drops,
through thoughts, our fantasy and reality
blend into our character which drags down to who we
are.
When all of it ends into one and one into many,
when we're the brightest in dark,
and darkest while being in the light,
we limit our true selves,
when we crave a starless night.
Our might, a shroud for hidden wars,
beneath these blankets, under egos' shade,
we search for a light we never met.
Wake up!! Just throw away this blanket,
time is slipping out of our hand.

We're mere raindrops who got lost in time,
yield to stillness, accept it, it's our end."

Let this curtain fall

"Let this curtain fall,
Let our story meet its end,
Let my heart forget,
The touch of your soft hands,
Let these dying sparks,
Ignite the eternal flame,
Let us shed our forms,
To forever be as one soul, one name.

It's dusk already,
Sun began to set deep within your eyes,
Listening to the hymn of love,
Stars started taking over the skies,
Our story, a timeless verse,
I would love to read it again,
For now letting this curtain fall,
But I promise, beyond life, we will meet again."

A Place I Long to Stay...

"*A space of peace in foothill's shade,*
Where snow-capped mountains are displayed,
A river's song, and forest's rain,
A quiet joy, to ease all pain.
A small hut, a woody shed,
Bonfires burning, that never fade,
No thoughts, nor worries,
Slow mornings, no hurries,
Beneath the stars I tranquilly sleep,
No bondage, no promises to keep,
Dreaming of a life, where present pales,
All I love is just to walk these trails,
Fresh life I breathe into my lungs,
Graced by nature's sunshine each day,
It's home, where sage's wisdom lies,
It's simple life for which I pray,
A place I long to stay."

Now There's Nothing I Want To Decide

"From side to side,
sought for a sight,
now there's nothing,
I want to decide.

These shadows grow,
as my greys shine,
even these scars of throes,
evanesce in time.

Fate smiles as,
it veils the arcane,
I carried away everything,
to rid myself of pain,
I set fire to all I blame,
hands in blood ashes shout my name.

War has no winners and it's true,
now, all that comes, I live it through,
after wars fought for myself,
I happily reside in letting it go.
If you're the next, wishing to change things your way,
tell me, when was the last summer you saw snow?"

www.ingramcontent.com/pod-product-compliance
Lightning Source LLC
LaVergne TN
LVHW021255200726
843509LV00012B/1675